Happiness

Unveiled

By

Helena Aramendia

HAPPINESS UNVEILED

A MHAR book
MHARbooks@gmail.com

All rights reserved
Copyright © 2010 by Helena Aramendia
Cover picture: Balancing stones © Olga Lyubkina
ISBN-13 978-0-9827979-1-4
ISBN-10 0-9827979-1-4

No part of this book may be reproduced or transmitted in any form or by any means, electronic or mechanical, including photocopying, scanning, recording, or by any information storage and retrieval systems, nor translated to any language without permission in writing from the author and publisher.

This book or its content can not be used as a center syllabus in workshops about happiness without permission in writing from the author and publisher.

Edited by Almut Metzroth and Mark Bateman.

I dedicate this book
to my soul mate, Mark.
With all my love and gratitude.

You are searching the world for treasure

But the real treasure is yourself.

If you are tempted by bread

You will find only bread.

What you seek for

You become.

Rumi (Hidden Music)

Contents

Preface 1

Note about the Book 5

Ch. 1 What Is Happiness and What It Feels Like 7

Ch. 2 The Forgotten Truth about Happiness 10

Ch. 3 Challenging Wrong Premises 15

Ch. 4 The Purpose of Happiness 20

Ch. 5 Love and Happiness 25

Ch. 6 Tool #1: Differentiating Blame from Responsibility 29

Ch. 7 Tool #2: Witnessing. Unidentifying with Your Body, Your Mind and the Life You Live 34

Ch. 8 Tool #3: Labels Are Good Only for Shopping 38

Ch. 9 Tool #4: Keeping the Right Perspective 43
Ch. 10 Tool #5: Gratitude 49
Ch. 11 Tool #6: Away with Guilt 54
Ch.12 Tool #7: Meditation
for Those Who Don't Meditate 62
Ch.13 Tool #8: Living in the Now 67
Ch.14 Simplify Your Life.
How to Use the Word No 71
Ch.15 Recognize, Enjoy and Share Your Happiness to
Make the World a Better Place 75
Epilogue: There Is a Faster Way to Do It 78
Happiness Unveiled 84
Recommended Reading 108

Preface

Do we really need another self-help book? That depends. Are you happy? If your answer is yes, you probably don't need this book, unless you are planning to buy it as a gift for somebody else. Chances are, however, that many of you have a different answer. In that case, you will be pleased to know that happiness is not a random attribute. It is a conscious choice, and, as such, it can be attained.

Sometimes we believe that important things in life, like happiness, love, or friendship, are blessings that came as celestial gifts. While this is partly true, it is also true that we are able to achieve those blissful gifts in a conscious and purposeful way.

Happiness is a choice. What does that mean? It may sound silly, since nobody would consciously choose anything different; who wants to be miserable? Truth is, we want to be happy but we often don't know how to go about it, or we try to achieve it following the wrong premises, or the wrong path.

Imagine that you want to be an architect. There are certain steps that you would need to take if you wanted to become one. Every step will be an active and conscious choice. Having the right grades, choosing the school, choosing to study instead of going out to party; choosing your projects, your reading materials; the way you spend your time, even your traveling, the clubs or associations you belong to; everything will lead to one result or another. You don't become an architect by enrolling into a law school. In a similar way, you don't achieve happiness by just hoping that it will happen.

Of all the necessary decisions in your pursuit of true happiness, by far the most important is the first one: Do you want to be happy? The rest will unfold, every step building upon the previous one, always while keeping your eyes on the prize.

This book has the intention of showing you the simplest possible way to happiness, without psychological, doctrinal or new-age jargon. I believe that simplicity is the key for success when learning new ways, and that is why I choose to focus on the basics that can take you to the happy life you deserve.

That said, let me also remind you that simplicity is not the same as easiness. For instance, it is simple to go out for a walk on a daily basis, or to go to the gym, but for many, it is not easy if they are not used to do it, or they have different habits.

Napoleon Bonaparte won many battles with a much smaller number of soldiers than the enemy fielded. It is said that he could do it by identifying his enemy's main force and concentrate most of his army on that objective.

I am following the same tactic with this book. I am focusing on the core points that will make the difference between being happy or not.

You will not find in this book a list of tasks that you need to do, think, believe, or long for in your life. Every person is different, but we all share the core of our human nature. Tips and exercises often don't work because they only modify external manifestations of a problem. By addressing the root issues, you will be able to find your own answers and your own tips. My intention in writing this book is to whisper to your soul, the aspect of you where we are more alike. I want to be a gentle reminder of the basic truth that your soul knows. It may be that you have forgotten this truth, because, like most of us, you are too busy surviving in an everyday more complex world.

Theories about spirituality, happiness and enlightenment have kept people away from these noble objectives because they often present the highest achievements as if they were daily routes for everybody to walk. The truth is, that to walk part of the path or to walk slowly, is always better than to remain asleep and not to walk the path at all. Absolute concepts and complex tasks can overwhelm you, so it is easier to deal with the idea of doing small improvements instead.

If you take a deep breath, relax and open yourself to new possibilities, I will show you the most simple and direct way to your true nature: happiness.

Note About the Book

I am not going to tell you anything that your soul does not know already. That is why I designed this book so you can read it two different ways: The pages at the end of the book have the essence, the core concept I want to share with you. You can read those pages by themselves to find the inspiration you need, or just to remember.

If those pages are not enough, or they do not yet resonate with you, the preceding pages have explanations of the basic concepts, so you can remember them more easily.

You did not become overnight the person you are now. When you think, feel, do or react in the same manner over and over, your reactions become part of you and create your reality. In the same way, to change your attitude to a better one requires you to insist on the new one. At first, it will take a conscious effort to think, to act, to react differently and to understand another point of view. However, once you see the reasons behind the alternative I propose to you, they will soon become second nature, as you will realize it is the natural way.

I know that everybody is a micro universe, with their own life, background, difficulties, experiences and point of view. My intention and my hope are that these pages are able to spread the sense of unity, peace and connection with the universe that I enjoy and that makes me happy.

Chapter 1

What Is Happiness and What It Feels Like

Happiness is not a perpetual state of peaceful and serene contentment. In fact, it would be unnatural and unrealistic to expect a total lack of conflict, pain, or sadness. Happiness is not attainable when you are in denial about feelings, but when you rise above them by understanding, accepting, or transmuting them.

For the purpose of defining a common understanding, let's analyze the meaning of being happy. You can consider happiness to be a long-lasting feeling of content and satisfaction that is not limited or related to a specific moment, event or cause. Happiness is not a joyful moment but a state of being. A happy person experiences sadness, anger, and upset; but because those are temporary states, they don't define the general way of being for that person. Therefore, happiness is not a mood; it is a way of life, an emotional state, a way of being.

Feelings are subjective, so people will have their own concept of how happiness should feel. Despite the limitations of language, you could say that the following are some of the common signs of happiness: having a feeling of peace, joy, everything being where it is supposed to be; feeling *at home* despite whatever is happening to you, around you, or in the world. That is what happy people would feel most of the time, regardless of the circumstances around them. If this does not get close to how you are feeling, I hope this book will be a good tool for you to achieve the happiness you deserve.

Happiness, like peace, is a state of the heart and the mind that permeates outward to daily life. A story illustrates that idea.

In a far-away country there lived once a king who wanted to have in his palace a perfect picture that represented peace. After looking at many, he chose two pictures. The first one represented a calm lake; it was truly a peaceful image. The lake was big and blue; its surface was totally still. The second picture was surprisingly different; it showed a waterfall between mountains. The water fell violently, splashing foam, roaring and creating whirlpools. Everybody at the palace was surprised to see the second picture, as they did not expect anything like it. They were even more surprised that the king chose that one. Once it was hanging on a big wall and the king and his people looked at it, they noticed why he chose it. Behind the falling water, in a crevice of the rock, there was an oasis of peace and love: a little nest with a small mother bird feeding her offspring. The king knew that true peace, like true happiness, is finding the calm that lives in the center of our hearts, regardless of what is happening around us.

Chapter 2

The Forgotten Truth about Happiness

You have to remember an important fact about happiness: Happiness is not something to achieve or to create but something to unveil, to tune into.

Happiness is a natural attribute, which resides inside you, next to your ability to love, to feel threatened or to fight for survival. Modern daily life has some positive benefits, but it has also some setbacks. Contact with the natural flow of nature is not the only ability that you are losing. A consequence of a fast-paced life is that you may tend to live most of the time with your focus on little thoughts about what is going on around you, ignoring or suppressing your instincts and some of your feelings. This is how you can become partially out of touch with your soul. Your natural state is for the most part contaminated with ideas, habits, cultural limitations, experiences or beliefs, which make it difficult for you to live in alignment with your true self. You could say that happiness is what you ignore while you narrowly focus on your daily happenings.

The following story is an example of how happiness is not a prize or something external to you, which you have to obtain either with luck or with effort. On the contrary, it is already inside you waiting to be recognized.

Once upon a time a beautiful girl lived in a small and peaceful village. She had lost her memory, so she spent her days wondering through the village, asking people if they knew her. She asked about her family, her name, her home, her history. She wanted to know who she was. At first, people were understanding of her situation. They comforted her, offered their friendship and their company. They offered jobs to her so she could make a living, but that did not satisfy her. She was barely surviving, unable to make a better life for herself. She felt the need to define herself through a name, a family, and a known origin. She became frustrated, bitter, and angry at the world, causing her illness and early death.

In a nearby village, another young girl lived without memory of who she was. Soon after she started questioning other people about herself without gathering any answers. She sat down under a tree, closed her eyes and felt sad for her situation. Feeling hurt, she cried for a long time, then sighed, and realized that she felt better. After taking some deep breaths, she became aware of her sadness and loneliness, but more importantly, of her body, her self, of being alive.

The girl got up, went back to the town and started to interact with the people, who comforted her, offered their friendship, their company, and jobs. She accepted all those gifts and felt grateful for them. Soon, she noticed that she felt better around some people and not around others. Working some jobs, the time seemed to pass much faster than doing others. Her favorite pastime was making bread. The smell, the touch, the magic going on while mixing a few simple ingredients pleased her. Without references to her life, she could now observe and notice her feelings about whatever was happening in and around her. She gravitated towards the people and the activities that made her feel better. Thus she became a bread maker, remained single, and settled in a tiny cottage by the river. She knew who she was. She was herself.

In this story, each girl's identity, the fact of knowing (or not) who she was, represents happiness. The first girl was so desperately trying to find it outside herself, that she became lost in the process grieving the lack of identity. The second girl, instead, took a simpler route: She unveiled her identity. By recognizing her feelings, experiencing that she *was*, she created her own references and claimed her identity.

You can do the same with happiness: you don't find it outside yourself in external references. You unveil it, for it is in you.

You may read about happiness or listen to well-intentioned people giving lists of things that you have to do in order to have a happier life. There is nothing wrong with doing things to improve your life, and many of those suggestions can have a positive impact. However, true happiness is not about achieving, it is about unveiling. It is not about working for it but about tuning in.

I do hope that the next pages will help you in tuning in to your own happiness, as I really would like to help you in this beautiful adventure that is unveiling the truth behind your life.

Chapter 3

Challenging Wrong Premises

Wrong Premise Number one:
I Will Be Happy When…

You think that you will be happy when you reach certain goals. Finding love, having a good job, achieving the economic or social level that you had planned, among others, are often the steppingstones you may feel you need in order to be fulfilled. The truth is that none of those goals are relevant or related to your happiness. There are endless examples of happy people with no apparent social success and, vice versa, unhappy people who seem to have everything they could possibly want in life, yet they remain dissatisfied.

The good news is that, because happiness does not depend on any of these factors, you don't need to wait for them to happen. You can start being happy right away. The moment is now. It is just a question of tuning in to it. Think about it this way: Humans are like TV receptors. Happiness will be a channel, which is already within your contract but one you never choose, because you are too busy watching other channels, featuring news, sports, movies....

Often you may find yourself deeply engaged in thoughts about events that upset you in the past, or possible outcomes that can potentially upset you in the future. When you do this, you are tuned to that specific channel, instead of tuning in to a happier one.

How do you stop unwanted thoughts? By putting others in their place. You cannot fight thoughts. The more you fight them, the stronger they become. They are like darkness: You can talk about it, complain about it, ask for it to disappear, but nothing will happen until you switch on a light. Unwanted thoughts will only go away when you replace them with other thoughts in your mind.

Wrong Premise Number Two:
Happiness Is Something That Happens, But It Does Not Happen to Everyone.

As stated before, happiness is not something that happens, but something that you tune in to. Therefore, it is not the privilege of a few. On the contrary, you, too, have the opportunity to be happy, in spite of your circumstances. You always have control over your life, whether directly through the actions you take, or indirectly with regard to your reactions when something unexpected happens.

You can take yourself to happiness in the same way in which you can learn how to cook, play guitar, make candles, play football, or drive a car. Like with any other skill, some people seem to be natural at it while others struggle somewhat, but all can learn how to tune in to it. It is simply a question of understanding the basics, having the will to do it, and focusing upon it. With most skills in life, practice makes perfect. Of course, in the process, relapse is normal. All changes require time. Be patient and understanding with yourself until you reach your goal. You are implementing new ways of looking at being and opening the door to new feelings.

As Erich Fromm said about love, happiness is also an art, and it can be learned. The pages you are holding are designed to help you in liberating your mindset, empowering you, and supporting you in your personal quest for happiness. You can do it if you want to. It is your choice, your decision.

Wrong Premise Number Three:
To Pursue Happiness Is Selfish.

It can seem selfish to pursue happiness while there is injustice, misery, pain and suffering in the world. On the other hand, there is a great opportunity for happiness in helping people in need. In any case, it is also a fact that the happier you are and the more you spread this feeling around you, the easier it will be to eradicate suffering for others.

You can look at happiness also from a pragmatic point of view. Everything in life is energy; everything has a specific vibration, whether you deal with something physical or something more subtle in nature, like an emotion. Therefore, happiness has a vibration. In the same way that a tuning fork tones musical instruments by resonance, the specific and strong vibration that qualifies as *happiness* will affect vibrations around it. Consequently, the more people vibrate in those high frequencies, the more people will be affected by that energy and will be able to be happy.

Chapter 4

The Purpose of Happiness

Although happiness is pleasant, it is not just a gift or something to feel for the sake of it. Happiness has a purpose. It is a navigational aid. It works like a Global Positioning System (GPS), telling us where we are in relation to our life plan. From this point of view, happiness is not an end in itself; on the contrary, it is a way of measuring how your life is unfolding.

Let's start at the point of incarnation. You incarnate for a reason. Your soul may have to learn, evolve, grow, guide others…. Whatever your purpose is, to incarnate in a physical body and to live a three-dimensional, physical life on earth is a great tool; so you design the master lines of your life, and you come to Earth.

Part of the incarnation process implies that you are not aware of your life plan or purpose. Free will is important in your growth as a human, but it is also a risk as your choices are not always in tune with your purpose. It is not easy to know what choices are better for you, what is in alignment with your original intention in incarnating. And here is where happiness enters the game.

Picture the continuous white lines painted on the sides and marking the limits of the roads As long as you see them, you know you are still on the path. If you cannot see them and the path is rough and uncomfortable, it means that you are off the track. Happiness is like the white lines. When you are happy, you know that you are on track in your life. When you are not, you need to make changes. It is really a simple device.

When you experience emptiness, a feeling of life not being enough, a sensation of you missing something important in your life, you are missing guidance from your soul. Somehow, you are not following your path. In the extreme, you may suffer from depression, if there is a big difference between the high energetic vibration of your soul, and the much lower vibration of your mental and emotional experience.

From this point of view, happiness is not an end in itself, but a way for you to know how close to, or how far you are from fulfilling your life purpose. You are not pursuing happiness for pleasurable and narcissistic reasons. You gravitate toward happiness because of a natural instinct, developed with the purpose of measuring if you are on the right path in your life.

It is not so strange that nature set you up with a pleasurable instinct to fulfill a task. One example of it, having to do in this case with your physicality, is sex. In order to ensure survival of the species, pleasure is associated with your reproductive instinct.

Another example, related to your physical body, is the feeling of well being that you experience when you are healthy and you look after yourself properly. As a physically healthy person you will feel good in your body: strong, flexible, energetic and balanced.

On the other hand, you have pain and sickness as as signs of physical dysfunctions. Both, pain and well-being, are ways to determine how you are looking after yourself. In that respect, they are both good, as they fulfill their purpose, if you listen to your body.

This insight takes you to the other side of happiness. Given that every coin has its reverse, the tail of happiness is crisis. A crisis is a tipping point of change, and as such, it is a point of growth and evolution. Nothing in nature is ever still; everything is in movement. Everything changes. Life, too, is dynamic. Through times of crisis, you arrive at happiness, and, eventually, at another crisis. The good news is that when you are able to see a crisis for what it is, —a moment of growth, a sign of a necessary change, an opportunity to find happiness— it becomes part of the process. Therefore, by definition, a crisis is part of happiness, even if it becomes uncomfortable or painful.

Many of you learn to look at life and happiness with the following image: you live surrounded by crisis, situations that don't allow you to be happy. You probably see happiness as a difficult goal.

Instead, this is the way things are: You are part of a bigger reality. Happiness is your natural state, and its purpose is to confirm that you are on the right track in your life. Crisis and problems are part of life and are necessary and useful to your growth. You can focus exclusively on them and feel like a victim, or you can choose to learn from them, to transcend them, to see them as the tools they are.

Speaking about states that are natural to you: Nothig is more natural in human nature than love. Thus, before we start reviewing the tools you can use in unveiling your happiness within, lets have a look at the role that love plays in this process.

Chapter 5

Love and Happiness

It is not possible to talk about happiness without mentioning love, as love is the connective tissue, the building block of life. Love is the energy that creates, permeates, and transcends everything. Romantic love, parental love, fraternal love, they are all partial aspects or manifestations of love. Those specific aspects are not absolutely necessary for you to be happy, but you definitely need to feel love if you want to tune in to happiness.

Endless numbers of books talk about love. Here, I just want to mention two points. First, notice that when I say *to feel love*, I mean to feel how you love, not how you are loved. To be loved is wonderful, but it is not the subject of this book. We are focusing on unveiling the happiness within you, and the first obstacle that you may encounter on your way is that you do not love, or you do not love enough.

The second point I would like to reflect upon is that the first subject to receive your love must be yourself. Love for self is the first and basic manifestation of the energy of love. If you do not love yourself, you cannot love anything or anybody. Furthermore, you cannot feel anyone's love towards you.

Unfortunately, many people will equate love of self or self-esteem with selfishness, egocentrism, or self-centering. Nothing could be further from the truth. Well-understood self-esteem is based upon the belief that you are one with the source of creation, you are worth and deserving of living a fulfilling life. You are not dependent on others to take care of your emotional needs. With a healthy self-esteem, you respect yourself more, and you respect others more; you value others, because you don't entertain the idea of some people deserving less love and respect than others. Finally and more importantly, you are in a position of loving and helping others around you, because you don't need to sacrifice yourself in order to feel validated, but you interact and help from a place of compassion and love.

In practical terms, self-love does not mean to ignore the needs of others. It means taking good care of yourself and, especially, coming to terms with the fact that, like everybody else, you are unique, irreplaceable, and lovable, no matter what. You are enough as you are. If you see attitudes in yourself that you don't like, you can do something to change them, but if *you* don't love yourself just as you are, nobody will. On the other hand, when you are able to love yourself, you are sending the message to the universe that you are able to love and you deserve to be loved.

You might have heard the little story about a very young orphan boy living in an impoverished and violent country in Africa. He was around eight or nine years old and had a sister who was less than three years old. They were in the streets of their dusty village when they received the visit of an international help agency. One of the workers was moved by the devotion and diligence of the older child looking after the little one despite his own very young age. The worker acknowledged that effort by saying that the agency was happy it could alleviate his load now. The man felt ashamed when the child, looking very surprised and somehow confused by the comment, smiled and just said, "Oh, she is not a load, she is my little sister." Only somebody with a good and healthy self-esteem and a heart overflowing with love, can look at such a responsibility not from a position of sacrifice but from a place of love.

Chapter 6

Unveiling Your Happiness

Regardless of your religious or spiritual beliefs, it is likely that we already agree about the fact that you are a soul incarnated in a physical body. Happiness belongs to this human aspect: the soul, the realm of the spirit; therefore, happiness is already in you. When you don't feel it, it means that your emotional life and your thoughts are focusing somewhere else; you are distracted. Thus you have to do a great deal of cleaning or uncluttering within yourself, until you are able to find it.

The following are some tools that I believe to be very useful in cleaning out your emotional reality.

Tool # 1: Differentiating Blame from Responsibility

Happiness Is A Choice

Let's assume that you are not happy and you would like to change that. By now, you already know that happiness is in you, but you need some help finding it and that is why you keep reading this book. You already checked on your self-esteem, on the love that you are able to feel for yourself and for others in your life. The next step is to know that whatever situation you are in now is not anybody's fault, not even your fault. There is nobody to blame. You need to let go and come to terms with the fact that happy people don't blame. You also need to know that it is your responsibility –and only yours- to move forward and to change whatever you need to change. That's it. Where there was blame, there will be taking responsibility for moving forward.

To be happy is a choice. A happy person will not rely on external circumstances to determine his or her feelings. You cannot always choose your external circumstances, but you can choose the way you react to them. Often, you might blame others for your lack of happiness, because they did or said something, and you reacted to that in a toxic way. It is your reaction to what they did, that is making you unhappy. Nobody has the power to make you happy or unhappy, unless you give them that power. It is time to stop blaming and start taking responsibility for your reactions, thoughts and feelings, as they are yours alone.

Consider this case: Berta was in her thirties, when her fiancé of four years left her for a woman he had met, only weeks before their wedding. Berta felt depressed, humiliated, and angry. Those feelings took over so that she was not able to establish a fulfilling relationship for more than five years.

Although it was not her fault that her fiancé left her, she was responsible for her reaction, for the way she dealt with it, and for the consequences that her response had in her life. As long as she kept insisting on the idea that she was the victim and he was the bad guy, she felt entitled to be bitter. However, she was the only one responsible for her lack of happiness. The question here is: do you want to be right —and keep being a victim—, or do you want to be happy?

Time and time again, the reason behind blaming others is to avoid feeling guilty when you really could blame yourself. Truth is that blame —whether it is towards yourself or toward others— is not necessary, desirable or useful. What you do with your mistakes is learn from them and move ahead. You let other people do the same. Mistakes, although they can be painful and have serious consequences, are part of life. If you hang onto them you are not able to continue with your life. Once blame is out of the equation, you can focus on your own reactions, and those are, definitely, your responsibility.

Here is another example of taking responsibility in your day-to-day life. The road is blocked, you are in a traffic jam and are late for an important appointment. You fall into a horrible mood. You spill the coffee and shout at your partner on the phone. Obviously, the initial situation is not your fault as you have nothing to do with the traffic situation. Your reaction, however, while still not your fault, is your responsibility. You can choose differently. You can observe yourself and consciously think that there is nothing you can do about being late, and use the time in a more positive way: keeping calm and making the best of those minutes in traffic.

Understanding this fact is important because it demonstrates the difference between taking control of our life and happiness, or being passive and hoping for the best. What is stopping you from making a better choice? Nothing but a habit, an automatic reaction. By witnessing those reactions you will be able to challenge them and make better choices.

People who have decided to be happy despite their circumstances stop blaming the world and take responsibility for their actions. Unhappy individuals, instead, lead empty and unhappy lives even if they don't have big challenges. Both groups are proof that happiness is a choice. It is your responsibility to make that choice.

Chapter 7

Tool #2: Witnessing.
Unidentifying With Your Body, Your Mind and Your Life

You are not your job, your financial or social position, not even your family or the relationships you have. You are what is inside you. Most people call it soul, but you can refer to it by any name or image you feel comfortable with.

When you are checking on how happy or unhappy you are, you will neither look at what you have or have not achieved, nor will you think about your job, your family, your health or your social life, because happiness belongs to the realm of the spirit, to your soul. Reflect solely on how you feel inside you, not in relation to anything external.

You will start by observing your body, feeling your comfort or discomfort. Are you tense, relaxed, hungry? Do you feel tired or full of energy? Are you hurting, numb, restless? Take some moments. Your focus should be on noticing all your sensations.

How is your body feeling right now from the inside out in relation to your physical body? Notice your skin, how is it in contact with the world outside? At this time, don't look at your body in terms of whether you like it or not, or what would you change. Notice how you inhabit your body: like a hermit crab inhabits its shell, only with a less flexible house exchange policy. However you may be feeling is not what matters at this point. What is important is the fact that by noticing how you feel *in* your body, you are differentiating yourself from it. Notice, too, the three different aspects of you when you are doing this exercise:

* Yourself, the one who is feeling whatever you are feeling;
* Your body;
* The observer, who is noticing what is going on.

If you are able to feel how you inhabit your body, you will realize that you are not your body. Your body is a vehicle, a physical support that you occupy. It is where you live, what you use to interact with the world, but it is not who you are. This awareness is the first step toward happiness; you achieved it by witnessing yourself.

In the same way, you can observe that your family life, your job, your financial situation or the way you live are directly or indirectly consequences of past choices you made; but they are not yourself. Whether those areas feel right or wrong to you, they are not who you are. They are what you have or what you live, but not who you are. Once you embody this truth, you will be able to tune in to the possibility of taking control and changing any part of your reality that does not resonate with who you are.

When you observe yourself, any aspect of yourself, you are witnessing. This exercise is an important tool for learning to know yourself better, and for changing anything that you would like to change in your life. The more you use this tool, the easier you can unidentify with everything that does not belong to your true nature. Witnessing is a tool for achieving real freedom. You need to know, however, how to react to what you witness, and that, you can explore in the next chapter.

Chapter 8

Tool #3: Labels Are Good Only for Shopping

Observing yourself, your feelings, your reactions, is a useful tool as you saw in the previous chapter. The secret to using it well is to leave judgment out of the equation.

You are accustomed to judging, to label everything as good or bad. A car accident is bad, a job promotion is good. Your spouse cheating on you is bad, winning the lottery is good. Those kind of labels are what we call *images* and they are ingrained in your mind, but they are not always true.

An old Zen story illustrates this fact. Once there was an old farmer whose horse ran away. The neighbors visited the farmer, feeling sorry for him. When they talked about his bad luck, he simply said, *maybe*. A few weeks later, the horse came back, bringing along a beautiful mustang. Everybody around the farmer was happy for him. His neighbors were saying how lucky he was. His answer was, *perhaps*. The week after, when the farmer's son was trying to tame the wild horse, he was severely injured. He had broken his leg and seriously wounded his foot. It took several weeks for him to recover, and, in the end, doctors could not save three of his toes. The boy could never run again. The farmer's wife was really upset, as were his neighbors. They all commented on how that was indeed bad luck. The farmer's response was, again, to smile and just say *perhaps*.

By now, the farmer's friends and neighbors were thinking that he was crazy, because they thought it unnatural to show such lack of emotion. It seemed that he did not care about anything, regardless of whether he received good or bad news. Six months later, the villagers understood better. The government had declared war to another country and was recruiting young boys for the army. When officers arrived at the farm, they saw that the boy could not run and decided not to take him. Needless to say, now the farmer's neighbors thought it was good fortune. Again the father reacted by saying *perhaps*. Finally, they understood what he meant.

In reality you cannot know, in the larger scheme of life, whether something is good or bad for your life journey. Life is complex, and destiny will take you where you need to go. Whether the path is a pleasant stroll or a tortuous labyrinth will depend mostly on your resistance toward it. In practical terms, I am sure that you have heard about the many lottery winners who have found misery and pain afterward, or about others who have found a leitmotif and happiness after a misfortune.

Facts per se are not good or bad. In the same way, you often understand or perceive other people's words or actions through your personal set of values. Consider the following true story.

A mature couple was going to cross a busy street. The gentleman, pointing to a specific moment and place between two cars passing on the road, said to his wife: "Cross through there." Nearby, a lady witnessing this moment, said to her daughter: "How lucky she is. See how he looks after her." A few minutes later, the wife crossing the street complained to a friend, "Can you believe it? He is so controlling that he tells me where to cross the street, as if I were a kid.

The witness was a widow who missed her late husband and felt lonely. She longed for him to take care of her, and that care was what she saw. The lady crossing the street, however, grew up with a rather severe and controlling father and she had issues with authority. The gentleman and caring husband liked to take control of things because he was self-confident. He devoted his life to looking after his wife, the lady he was trying to help. All of them were correct but partial in their judgments. The interesting part was to observe how something so ordinary affected both women. One did a trip to nostalgia road, the other became angry. In the end, their reactions were in their minds, for the gentleman had only said: "Cross through there."

When you release your need for judgment and control, you find freedom.

When you cease judging and labeling situations as positive or negative, learning to ride them all with the same attitude of trust, you are changing your perspective in life. Keeping the right perspective means that you focus on the big picture, considering a larger reality than what your senses are immediately presenting to you. This theme is further explored in the next chapter.

Chapter 9

Tool # 4: Keeping the Right Perspective

When you face daily problems, you focus upon the narrow reality of something developing differently from your plans or desires. As you already saw, you might have the tendency to immediately label events or experiences as good or bad, based upon a very poor and narrow point of view. However, when you broaden your perspective, you can see that setbacks are often blessings. After all, since you are not the life you are living, everything serves a higher purpose.

Your higher purpose in life is not based on religious beliefs but on the path of your soul. Reality in your physical experience will be modified as needed in order to fulfill that purpose.

If you play chess, you know that the objective of the game is to achieve a checkmate; in the process, some pieces will be sacrificed but all serve a higher purpose. If you have children, you also know that the tears you wipe from their little faces when they receive vaccinations are the price to pay for protection from disease. It is easy to see the bigger picture in those two mundane examples. You focus on the final objective and see those little sacrifices as irrelevant. Your life is more complex, so it is not always easy to understand some situations that you face in life, those which bring pain and suffering. You incarnate with the general purpose of growth and evolution, through individual specific challenges. To fulfill that purpose, you need to have certain experiences. At times, you listen to your soul and naturally follow the path you designed for yourself. Yet, often, you are oblivious to that path. Life then gives you wake-up calls. Those calls get louder if you keep ignoring them. You have to keep in mind that bigger perspective.

To remember that everything happens for a reason is not enough to overcome the pain or the upsetting moments in life. Changing your perspective, though, can help to make both mellower. Check the following way of achieving this goal.

Start by being aware of your pain, your anger, or any other feeling that you would like to overcome.

Now, imagine that you are looking at yourself through a video camera. See yourself while you are feeling that pain. In that way, you are now both, the one that observes and the one that is been observed.

Afterward, you may see yourself from a greater distance, including your room in that vision, and people in it. You see the house, the neighborhood, the city, you see your country, your planet.

Finally, you can go one step further and see yourself not just in one location but also in a particular moment in time: this year; a few years earlier; when you were younger; when you were young; when you were born. You can see into the future, too: in a few months; in a few years; all your life. Your life in this time and space is really a blink in a speckle of land in space, but you, the observer, are still there, bigger than time, bigger than space, able to observe the tiny and fragile reality of a human incarnation. There is divine precision in the apparent chaos of life. The experiences you live have the purpose of teaching you necessary lessons, or facilitating your growth. Suffering will pass, because it is only a reaction to an event and it is conditioned by your thoughts and your personal belief system. The part of you that is observing, on the other hand, is eternal, growing and evolving; it is shaped by the events lived in its incarnation. Acceptance of this fact results in the ability to transcend suffering and to grow.

As you can see, an intense pain will probably not disappear even from this very broad perspective, but chances are that the upset created by your husband not closing the tube of toothpaste, as well as most other upsets in your daily life will fade. Keeping the right perspective is important when you are unveiling your happiness. It means that you are aware of the fact that you are part of a much bigger reality, and how unimportant and trivial most events are around us.

The story of five blind men living in a little village in India demonstrates perspective.

One morning, the five blind men were sitting in the fields, when a little boy came running. "An elephant! An elephant!" he cried. The five blind men were excited because they never came near an elephant before. They managed to gather around the animal. By touching it, they tried to understand what an elephant was. After a while, the first man, who was touching the tusks, said, "The elephant is cold, hard, and very smooth."

The second one, who had been touching a leg, said, " No, the elephant is thick and round like a tree." The third man, touching the ear, said, "No, the elephant is flat, light and tall."

The forth one, who had been touching the tail, said, "You are all wrong; the elephant is long and thin, like a rope."

Finally, the fifth man, who had been feeling the flank, said, "You are all wrong, because the elephant is hard, big, rough, and flat like a wall."

The men started a fight, as every one of them was absolutely sure of what he had felt, and it was clear for each of them that the others were wrong. Fortunately, the little boy from the village ended the fight by explaining that they all noticed a different part of the animal, and that every one of them was right, but only partially.

Reality was bigger than what they could perceive, and that is what happens to you most of the time.

The blind men in the story were grateful to the boy for the explanation, and gratitude is the next great tool you will learn about.

Chapter 10

Tool #5: Gratitude

Gratitude is important in unveiling your happiness. Since your feelings determine your vibration, gratitude is a doorway to a better reality. As a positive feeling it also interacts with your environment, sending a distinctive message of recognition and appreciation. Gratitude requires for you to be open and able to receive and recognize that you are receiving.

You can arrive at this conclusion after a simple observation of life. For instance, if you are the cook at home, what dish will you prepare more often, the one that is enthusiastically praised and gratefully enjoyed by your family, or the one that ends up feeding the pets? The consequence for people who are appreciative at the table is that they usually eat better.

When are you more careful remembering special occasions and choosing gifts, when recipients show appreciation for them or when they systematically ignore them? Gratitude is a feeling that sends a message to the universe: I like this, I deserve this. What's more, lack of gratitude also sends a message: I don't care; it doesn't matter; I didn't notice it; I don't deserve it. And the universe always responds.

In terms of energetic vibration there is also an explanation: When your thoughts are positive, you feel better, and your vibration increases. Unlike electric energy, in bio-energy equal attracts equal. As a result, you attract people, objects, and events of similar vibrations. In other words, whatever you focus your attention on becomes stronger and bigger. If you direct your attention to the things you don't like, or you don't feel grateful for, they will grow more important and will take more space in your reality. On the other hand, when you feel grateful, you are focusing your attention on what you feel grateful for, and that is what will grow in your life.

One of the authors whose books I like to recommend to my friends and customers is Dr. Masaru Emoto. As a healer I am totally aware of the effects of thoughts, feelings and words in the physical world. As a happy person who cultivates gratitude I know of its effects in my life. Nevertheless, it is really stunning to be able to see with your own eyes, in a physical and tangible way, the effects that gratitude, as well as other words and feelings, can have in water.

In Dr. Masaru Emoto's book, *The Hidden Messages in Water*, you can read that water can be programmed, or can carry information. He demonstrates this by taking pictures of frozen drops of water before and after being exposed to different sounds, written or spoken words, or feelings. Dr. Emoto found that love and gratitude form the most beautiful crystals, regardless of the language.

If gratitude can create a crystal like this

from a drop of water like this

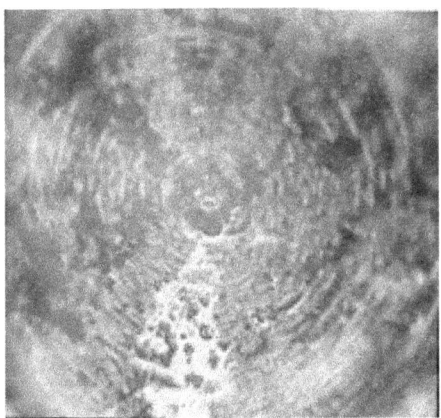

and you are 70% water, you have to acknowledge that thoughts, words and emotions shape your reality.

Another reason for the importance of taking the time to feel grateful is that taking time slows down your path and makes you be present, even if only for a moment. Happiness compares to an impressionist masterpiece made of countless small strokes.

You are not pretending to be illuminated or putting your life on hold, while you behave like pure spirit. On the contrary, a healthy aspiration is to have many moments during your day when you are present and aware. Gratitude means you are not taking for granted the sun, the light, the air, your body, your family, and so many other things that nourish and support your life.

If you don't believe you have anything at all you can be grateful for, sit down calmly, and think again. There is always something that you can appreciate. As you practice more, you will recognize more reasons to be grateful. If you are skeptical, just give it a sincere try.

Chapter 11

Tool # 6: Away with Guilt.

You are cleaning your emotional reality in order to facilitate tuning in to happiness. One of the most wildly accepted and most unnecessary pieces of baggage you tend to carry with you is guilt. How can you deal with it in a purposeful and healthy way?

From a spiritual point of view, *holding on to guilt is a burden*, a toxic waste in your mind. If blaming others gets in the way of connecting to your soul or true nature, blaming yourself endlessly does the same. When you hold on to your guilt, you are wasting your time, as this prevents you from loving or feeling grateful; in other words, from being happy and carrying on with your life. Guilt is a low-vibration energy and will attract more of the same. Notice that I did not say *guilt is a burden*, but *holding on to guilt is a burden*, as there is a big difference. You can compare it to the start button of your car: useful for only a moment; or to salt: good in only small amounts.

The only purpose for guilt is to show you who you really are in terms of whatever you are feeling guilt for. For instance, only if you are honest, will you feel guilt when you act in a dishonest way; only if you are truthful, will you feel guilty for lying. Psychopaths are the ones who will not show any remorse, guilt, or repentance for their actions. Therefore, guilt is showing your true nature, behind where your actions took you. Feeling guilt will make you realize that you are not what makes you feel that way, and so you can rise above it. When you accept that truth and focus on the reality of who you are behind and above your personality, you can connect to your soul and are also one step nearer to unveiling happiness.

Once you notice that your earlier choices were not in alignment with your true nature, guilt is not necessary any more; to hang on to it would be a burden for you. When you realize the extent of your actions, you repent, and you give compensation if possible. The next step is to forgive and to learn from your errors. This process implies that you let completely go of your guilt. Your problem arises when you insist on clinging onto guilt, instead of letting it go.

Letting go of emotions, be they perceived as good or bad —especially if they are bad— often feels like a difficult task, because you don't have your mind trained to do so. Once you learn it, however, it is a blessing and a liberating skill. The process is accomplished in two steps: First, you have to *realize* that you are holding on to guilt and *decide* without a doubt that you want to get rid of it. Second, you must focus your mind on a different subject. If it is difficult for you to stop thinking about that specific issue, a good choice is usually to decide what is that you will do differently when the occasion arises again, or how much better your life is going to be now that you understand your mistake. Focus on how much better you can feel from now on, because you have learned a lesson. Whenever you are ready to give total closure, just *focus* on the other areas of your life in that moment.

If you think your mind is the one in control, you have to challenge that thought. You must be the one in control of your mind, as your thoughts define your reality.

A little Zen story gives you an example about letting go. Two Buddhist monks were walking near a river, when they saw a distressed beautiful woman. She needed to cross to the other side, but the current was too strong for her. One of the monks, without thinking twice, carried the lady on his back, and the three arrived safely at the other bank. A few days later, the other monk could not keep his feelings to himself any longer and angrily said: "You know we can't have contact with females. Why did you do it?" to which the first monk responded: "I left the girl there. Are you still carrying her?"

Often, you feel guilt without a reason. Linked with feelings of inadequacy and lack of self-esteem, guilt is a way to punish yourself for not reflecting an idealized version of yourself, which you hold as the correct template for how you should be. Self-acceptance and a healthy dose of self-esteem will get rid of those guilt-for-no-reason moments. You probably feel guilt for the most bizarre reasons, from eating chocolate to having sex, not exercising enough, not giving enough to charity, not listening enough, not spending enough time with somebody.... You may even feel guilt for what other people feel. If they cry, if they are unhappy... but their feelings are not your responsibility. That kind of guilt is a redundancy and a negative burden to carry. It is a way of punishing yourself without making you a better or a happier person.

Other times, even when you may feel guilty about a more specific and negatively perceived fact, you have to remember two considerations. You already know you cannot label things as good or bad, because you do not have enough information about the big picture. You are not aware of the broader reality, so you are in no position to determine if the outcome you are regretting was, in fact, the best of other possible realities, despite circumstances. Let another story illustrate this point of not being aware of the broader reality.

Once upon a time, a playful angelical spirit called Asiel was enjoying eternity, when a member of its soul family came with a question. "What is suffering? I can't imagine that feeling".

Asiel, always willing to help, responded with a proposal. "If you want, I can help you with that. Because I love you deeply, and there are no words that can describe such a feeling, we both need to incarnate as humans. I am willing to incarnate with you, so I would be able to facilitate that learning by creating the deepest pain you can face."

With that agreement, the spirit that didn't know about suffering incarnated first. A few years later, Asiel incarnated as her son. When Asiel was ten years old, he died in a car accident, leaving his mother in total despair. In that way, he fulfilled his promise to her. The person who caused the accident never forgave himself for killing the boy. However, all events respond to a bigger scheme. Against guilt, it is useful to be humble, and to remember that you are part of a much bigger reality.

The second consideration about guilt is that even in the worst case scenario, even if it were true that you purposefully committed a terrible act —whether you can fix it or not— guilt has no reason to be present, but will bring negative consequences. Remember to keep the right perspective. You are an incarnated soul. Your personality did something that you experience as regrettable, so you learn from it, offer the best possible compensation given the circumstances, and forgive yourself. From here on, if you keep turning to guilt without letting go of it, you are losing perspective by focusing on your narrow mind, which is the one reminding you of how terrible you are. Moreover, you do not love yourself, because when you love, you forgive. If you think that because of what you did you don't deserve forgiveness or happiness, you are wrong. Again: guilt is a low-vibration energy that will keep you anchored in a petty corner of your personality, from where you can have only small thoughts. When you dare to truly connect with your soul, you will find an endless ocean of love, able to dissolve the darkest feelings. Your soul is the part of the divinity that lives in you. Your soul is only love, so it can only love.

    How can you connect with your soul? Whenever you feel ready to keep reading, peruse the next chapter.

Chapter 12

Tool #7: Meditation for Those Who Don't Meditate

As part of the creative process of this book, I contemplated the importance of meditation, as well as various methods for it. I am also keeping in mind my intentions and the spirit of this book: simplify, don't suggest many practices, routines or exercises and don't get dogmatic. That said, I believe in my heart that I can present a meditation that can be easily adopted even for those of you that have never considered it previously and that have no intention of meditating. Bear with me a little more.

It is well-known and well-documented that the practice of meditation has many benefits at a physical, mental and emotional levels. It is easy to find a variety of techniques, teachers, books, videos or applications, all suggesting different ways to meditate, for new as well as seasoned practitioners. In terms of happiness, the practical and more direct benefit of meditation is that it helps with achieving the mind control that you need in order to work with your thoughts. Witnessing or letting go of negative thoughts, for instance, are skills that you can master more easily if you meditate, therefore, I strongly recommend that you consider the possibility of exploring the many choices you have around, and start practicing meditation regularly.

However, I am acutely aware of the fact that starting a meditation practice is not even remotely conceivable in the near plans of many of my readers. If you are one of them, this chapter is for you. I am going to try to extract the essence of meditation, so you can benefit from it, even if you don't practice it. Think of it like having meditation pills.

Every morning, the very first second that you wake up, just when you become aware of being awake and being in your bed, stop right there. Before you start having any thoughts or any moves, be also aware of who you are. Notice how your body feels. Notice that you are already witnessing yourself. Recognize your true self, your spiritual self, the one that you really are: not your name, physical appearance, or occupation, but your soul; just see it, recognize it for a moment. Grasp that second of silence and stillness before your mind starts its incessant chatter. Own that infinite instant before your attention goes to life outside of you. That second is the magic door to your soul, if you were looking for one, so make it longer. Another second, perhaps a few more…. There is just you, in the present moment, the Creator is with you because you are one with creation. This is a long moment of perfect stillness. That second has the key to your happiness. No worries, no thoughts, no plans. Just for a moment. Only awareness of your own presence in the moment. Feel your breathing. The more often you can feel that second, the more aware of your consciousness, and the happier, you will be. Moreover, you will be thankful for that moment of meditation and the peace and perspective it brings to your life. That will be your first thought of the day: noticing that you are feeling grateful not just for that moment and for life in general, but for everything else you can be grateful for. Once you get used to it, it will become the best part of your day, and you will find yourself taking that meditation pill and having gratitude thoughts often during the day.

That's it. Done. You can go on with your day. You will want to repeat this process just before you fall asleep. When you get proficient at this practice, do it during the day, at any moment, until you get used to do it often. Meditation in this form may take only a few seconds. It will not give you a full membership to the meditators club, but it will give you a seasonal pass with rights to many benefits.

The reason for meditation is to bring your awareness from whatever is outside of you, to who you are inside, so you will be able to connect to your soul, and to control your mind. This simple practice will set you on your way to achieving both. If having a regular meditation practice is like doing the path in a limousine and with a professional guide with you, this little practice is like doing the path walking and following the road signs. Slowly but surely, it will take you there as long as you keep moving one foot in front of the other. The only requirement, the only secret, is to do it. You will notice its benefits only if you practice. You can do it. You have all you need, and you will love it.

Chapter 13

Tool #8: Living in The Now

In spiritual and new age circles it is very fashionable to talk about *living in the now*, and you can find great books about the subject. It is a concept born from the fact that we only have the present moment and that is what we have to focus on, in order to take control of our life and live it fully. Personally, I totally agree with the idea behind it; moreover, I pledge on the many positive changes that this practice will bring to your life; but being myself a very practical person, I wanted to simplify it for you.

When you actually observe your thoughts during the day, you realize that most of the time they are either reenacting something that has already happened, or projecting to a possible future. Living in the now means that you focus your attention in the present moment instead of constantly recreating the past or imagining the future.

A classical Zen expression says, "When you wash rice, just wash rice." It refers to your focus upon the present tasks, not only giving relevance to what you are doing in the moment and making it more purposeful, but also keeping your mind free of clutter. When you think about it, what are the alternatives if you are not thinking about the rice? Your mind is like a monkey, constantly chitchatting. When you are not totally focusing on the now, you are not fully present, engaged and able to enjoy it, which is, in itself, enough reason to be focused. Moreover, ideas that seem to have a life on their own also distract you. Remembering what somebody said or did to you, is reliving it again. If this recurrent past event is perceived by you as negative, or hurtful, you are avoiding closure and healing. You are not letting go. If you are thinking about something in the future, the risk is that it is an opportunity to let fears inside your mind. The more you think about certain events, the more you can imagine going wrong. You know how creative you can be in this department.

The challenge you can face with this practice of living in the moment is that it does not always seem practical. At times, you need to think about the past in order to understand situations and to avoid repeating mistakes, or, if you are recreating a happy moment, in order to keep that positive feeling with you. Other times, you need to plan for the future if you don't want to constantly improvise. Even if you are a spontaneous and flexible person that likes to go with the flow, you will need a certain amount of planning to make your life easier and more predictable. Besides, visualization is a powerful technique for creating and manifesting the future we imagine, and implies taking some time from the *now* to project the future, so my recommendation for you to unveil your happiness is this: you don't need to live in the now every moment, but you need to be fully present every moment and focusing completely on whatever you are doing. You will find that everything is more relevant. You will notice that engaging fully in your routine is a source of joy and pleasure. What is more important, you will find it so much easier to control your mind, and, consequently, your feelings.

Chapter 14

Tool #8: Simplify Your Life. Use The Word *No*

You already saw the core steps you need to unveil happiness. They will help you to clean up emotional clutter. The tools you have now, will help with most of what you can do to unveil happiness. However, you can also change some patterns in your daily life. Certain facts, habits, situations, or environmental conditions can be impediments to a more fulfilling life. Those factors, although less relevant (despite appearances), are often easier to manage and should not be overlooked. Every one of you has different circumstances, so I am not going to be able to comment on all the possible aspects of life that could be holding you back in terms of happiness. A good life coach can help you to determine the aspects of your daily life that you can reconsider, if you feel that you are too close to determine what may be changed. Yet, there is something that is very general in society, and you must learn how to challenge: the fact that life is getting too complicated.

It seems that you should be able to enjoy life more calmly and have more time for yourself, since every day there is more technology to ease your life. All kind of devices, machines and appliances enable you to accomplish more tasks faster. Nevertheless, it is likely that everyday you feel more stressed out, and complain about lack of time. Even children are starting to suffer from stress.

The solution is to declutter your life as much as you clean your emotional realities. There is not only too much holding on to fear, too much guilt, too little gratitude or too little love, but also too many activities and demands during the day. As you clean your emotional life, you will notice that it is easier to create more simple and fulfilling days.

One way to start is by questioning your daily activities and deciding whether they are truly necessary. At times it may not cross your mind that you can just say no to a meeting, a party, a job, or any other kind of event. You may judge yourself, feeling selfish, unsociable or lazy if you don't go. You may give in and manage to fit in yet another appointment. However, the world will not stop rotating if your kids play more and have one less extra-curricular activity. The floor will not fall from under your feet if every now and then, you can write in the dust of your furniture. Your company will not go bankrupt if you end your workday on time. The secret is to decide what your priorities are and then focus upon them. A story about how to prioritize can help with this concept.

    A teacher was giving a lecture at college. On the table, he had a big empty vase and beside him a very big bag. He silently took big stones from his bag and filled up the vase. He asked the students "Is the vase full? Their answer was yes. Next, he took small stones, and put them inside the vase. The stones were filling the spaces between the big ones. He repeated his question. They, again, answered yes, the vase was full. The teacher reached for another bag and started to pour sand in the vase. He asked again if the vase was full. Exasperated, his students answered affirmatively. At last, he took a jar of water from the bag, and completely filled the vase. "Now, it is full," he said.

The secret to managing your time better is to consider what our big stones are. If you put the small stones first, there will not be space for the big ones. More importantly, there is always space for water.

Water represents your spiritual life, your moments for connecting to your soul, your moments for giving a meaning to anything you do. Those little seconds of mind silence that you read about in chapter twelve, they are the drops of water. Those drops are your love, which surround every stone and every grain of sand, fulfilling every one of your days. And it is okay to say no to anything that does not fit in the vase, because if it is already full, what is the point in feeling bad for the stones that could not fit in?

Whenever you are confronted by something that does not fit in your life, you can say no.

Chapter 15

Recognize, Share and Enjoy Your Happiness To Make The World a Better Place

Unveiling happiness is something that may probably take you a while. Although the process itself is simple, it is not always easy to challenge your images and to consider different ways of looking at things. However, at the end of the day, remember that it is just a question of making a shift, like when you change the channel on the TV. Happiness was already there but you were too distracted to notice. The tools you have now will help you in seeing it, unveiling it and recognizing it. Once you tune into it, do not keep it for yourself. Like good food, it tastes even better when shared with others.

Humans are like cells in a complex organism: individual parts of a whole. In the same way that cells form tissues, organs and systems, humans are part of families, communities, societies, the human race, and finally, a whole entity with our mother earth.

Whether you like it or not, and no matter how individualistic you may be, the fact is that every human is connected to this whole body. Individual happiness, then, is like having healthy cells in an organism. The greater the number of healthy cells working in an harmonic and balanced way, the healthier the organism is. The more people are happy, the better the world functions. Every human, without exception, is an integral part of the whole. The world needs your specific talents, your dreams, your individual attributes, what you like and what you dislike about yourself. Without you, it would not be the same. You have the responsibility to be happy because you are never alone, and you are like a piece in a puzzle. Without you, it would never be complete.

You don't need to be a hero or to do anything extraordinary. You just need to be yourself. You cannot make anybody happy, but you are responsible for being happy yourself. Often, when you are around people who are suffering, you cannot do anything to solve their situation, but if you are happy, you love them and you are with them, they will feel better. Happiness is infectious; it will spread around you because it will resonate with other people's souls, reminding them of its presence.

Be as happy as you can and spread it as far as you can, and you will be healing the world.

Epilogue

There Is a Faster Way To Do It

Happiness is a natural state when living in alignment with your life purpose. It is a peaceful feeling, because peace is what you experience when you connect to your true self or soul. Peace feels like being in the eye of the storm: a place of perfect calm and stillness. The awareness of that peace is happiness.

If you look back through the book, in all sections you have been reading about awareness. When you meditate, when you take charge of your feelings or use any of the other tools from the book, you will notice that they have something in common: they require awareness. The fact that you witness yourself and you become aware is what really makes the difference. Think about it. If someone puts one million dollars in your bank account it will not make any difference to you until you become aware of it. Your thoughts about it will trigger a reaction and a feeling; however, it is not the money that will bring you joy, but the awareness of it and your thoughts about what the money can do for you. In terms of your real life, it is the awareness of being part of a much bigger reality that puts you in tune with your happiness.

You came into this world with your soul purpose. You don't need to know what it is necessarily. You can follow it by following your dreams, because they are your soul's language. If you are not happy, you are not following your heart. Among six billion people, there is only one of you, unique and different, like every snowflake. The world needs your talents, whatever they may be. The world does not need for each individual to be the One, the Illuminated, the Savior. You don't need to be perfect. You just need to be fully yourself. The world needs each one of you to be awake, which means that you are aware of your spiritual nature.

At the start of the book I stated that unveiling happiness is a simple process, as it exist already in you. You just need to tune in to it. I never said, however, that you have to see la vie en rose from now on.

Sadness, tears, anger, anxiety, fear, upset as well as joy, contentment, excitement, and the full range of human emotions are signs of aliveness. They are as good and as necessary as the air you breathe. Happy people can submerge themselves in any of those emotions when the moment arrives, and yet, they can overcome and rise above difficulties by keeping centered in their hearts, knowing that the bad moments, like the good ones, will pass, but they themselves will remain.

    For instance, a friend of mine lost her job. As a single mom with two children, a dog and a mortgage, she could panic and become depressed with the situation, especially in times of a weak economy and a high unemployment rate. She could also feel bitter and angry about the unfairness of it. Instead, she is enjoying the activities that she could not pursue while she was working so many hours. She spends more time with her family, looks after herself better, exercises, enjoys more time with her friends, and is considering which direction she would like to go professionally. Certainly, she is not pleased for the loss of her job but is thankful for the free time she has and for the fantastic opportunity to do all those things. She trusts that this change in her life is happening for a reason. She is enjoying every minute of it, and, at the same time, is diligently sending out job applications. Best of all, she is applying only for the positions that come close to what her heart is longing to do. She is in alignment with her soul, letting life take care of her. She made an admirable choice seeing a difficult situation as an opportunity to improve her life. Unfortunately, we all know people who lapse into anxiety, or even depression, due to the anger and above all, the fear caused by similar situations. My friend has moments when the fact of her financial situation's stalemate comes to her mind, but as soon as she notices the negative thoughts she pushes them away by focusing on positive ones.

    This book opened with challenging some premises. You saw that happiness is a choice and also a way to determine if you are doing with your life what you came here to do. As you worked through fifteen chapters of the book, you saw that you can de-clutter your emotional life, realizing that happiness is your birthright and that you can tune in to it right now. You saw that you have to love more, to love unconditionally. As mother Teresa said, "Love until it hurts, don't stop loving."

You also learned not to blame circumstances any longer but to take full responsibility for your reactions, for your thoughts and for your happiness. You learned that you are not your life and to stop judging. Now you look at situations from a much broader perspective, feel grateful and push aside guilt and fear. You purposely feel connected to your heart, the source of your life. You take the time every day to feel oneness with all creation. You simplify your life and live in the moment. You share happily what you have found on your path; but the process took a while. What could make it faster?

Sometimes you need to take a longer path, because it is the only one you are able to walk, and that is okay. Other times, you take it because you don't know any better. For those of you who want to take a shortcut, try the fast path: when you are aware of your soul, you experience peace. In that peace, you can receive your soul's guidance. When you follow this guidance, you unveil happiness. That is what it means to be in alignment with your soul. You can be happy if you are able to remember that you are like a drop of water. It does not matter what part of the water cycle you are in, watering plants, singing in a fountain, diluting dirt, or being evaporated and disappearing, you will always end up enjoying being with the dolphins because that is in your nature. You are part of the creation and the Creator, as they are one, and that is the higher truth that can overpower any other thought. When you accept that truth and feel it in every cell, you don't need to search for happiness any more. Every second of your life that you allow yourself to embody that reality, you are able to transcend everything else, and you are tuning in to your happiness.

HAPPINESS UNVEILED

*You don't need to wait for anything.
Happiness is in your heart now, even if you didn't notice it yet.
Dare to see it.
Dare to unveil the peace that lies in the center of your spirit.
It is deep and immense like an ocean.*

You are a spiritual being experiencing life in a physical body.
When you were born, you started this experience by limiting yourself to a three-dimensional frame.
When you die, you return to your eternal reality.

Happiness is a guidance device for your life.
It is simple.
When you are not happy, you know you have to find your path again.
When you are happy, you know you are where your spirit needs to be.

Your path is the path of the spirit.
Your true nature is love.
Happiness is a reminder of this truth.
Only loving and being aware of your nature
will enable you to unveil the happiness that
lies within you.

There is only one choice in life:
love, or fear.

*When you blame others for the way you feel,
you are giving them power over you.
Empower yourself by taking responsibility
for your feelings and your thoughts.*

You are not your family,
you are not your job,
you are not your body.
You are not the life you are living.

You are the love that you give.

There are not good or bad situations.

There are situations.

*Beauty, as well as ugliness,
is in the eyes of the observer.*

When a big storm batters your house
in the valley,
only from the top of the mountain
can you see the nature of the storm
without getting hurt.

What are you feeling guilty for?
Can you do anything about that?
If you can, do it and send your guilt away,
as it is of no use to you.
If you can't, send your guilt away,
as it is of no use to you.

How do you send your guilt away?

Guilt is just a thought.
Put a better one in its place.

Meditation is the ability to enjoy the magical silence of your mind.

*Studies have proved that meditation
has numerous tangible benefits for
your body, your mind and your spirit.
However, you will notice those benefits
not by reading about them, but only by
meditating.
You may as well start right now.
Just close your eyes,
and enjoy the breath that keeps you alive.*

*Don't get caught in the jungle of your
daily worrying, in the incessant chatting
of your mind.
Instead, dare to ignore them for
just a moment
and tune in to the beauty of your heart,
where happiness lives.*

The past is just a thought.
It does not exist any more.
The future is just a thought.
It does not exist yet.
Only the present exists.
As a present, it is really a gift.

You only have this moment.
Make it last by living it fully.
Live it fully by being aware of it.

These are the tools that you have for your life's trip

A GPS, called happiness, so you can tell whether you are lost or on the right path;
A bright light, called love, so you can see the reality of what is in front of you;
An endless amount of currency, called gratitude. The more you use it, the more you will acquire whatever you need for your trip;
A communicating device, called Silence, because only in the silence of your mind will you find the right direction and advice.
A master key, called forgiveness, because only when you forgive yourself and others, will you set yourself free.
As many mirrors as you need along the way, because every situation and every person you find on your path is reflecting one part of yourself.
To carry all, you have a backpack called awareness.

Your Most Natural State

*Never underestimate
The power of wonder, joy and love.
For that is your most natural state,
and one that you are always in.*

*You are always in this state,
Even though you may not be
consciously aware of it in the moment.
You may be narrowly focused upon a life issue.
But what is a life issue, compared to the vastness?*

From Seeds of the Spirit 2002, © by BarbaraBrennan

Recomended Reading

Brennan, Barbara. *Hands of Light*. New York, Ny: Bantam Book, June 1988.

Dahui, Yuanwu, Foyan, Yuansou, Linji and others (selection by Thomas Cleary). *Zen Essence*. Boston, Ma: Shambhala Publications, Inc, 1989.

The Dalai Lama and Howard C. Cutler, M.D. *The Art of Happiness*. New York, Ny: Riverhead Books, 1998.

Emoto, Masaru. *The Hidden Messages in Water*. Hillsboro, Or: Beyond Words Publishing, Inc, 2004.

Hicks, Esther and Jerry. *Sara, Book 1*. California: Hay House, April 2007.

Lipton, Bruce, PhD. *The Bilology of Belief, unleashing the power of consciousness, matter, & miracles*. Santa Rosa, Ca: Mountain of Love / Elite Books 2005.

Pert, Candace, PhD. *Molecules of Emotion, the science behind mind-body medicine.* New York, Ny: Scribner (Simon & Schuster), 2003.

Rumi. *Hidden Music.* China: Barnes & Noble by arrangement with HarperElement, 2009.

Three initiates. *The Kybalion.* New York, Ny: Penguin Group, 2008.

Tolle Eckhart. *A New Earth.* New York, Ny: Penguin Group, October 2005.

Trott Susan. *The Holy Man.* New York, Ny: Riverhead Books, 1995.

www.ingramcontent.com/pod-product-compliance
Lightning Source LLC
LaVergne TN
LVHW041631070426
835507LV00008B/559